Fundamental concept of linux for newcomers

Introduction to Linux 3
   What is Linux? 3
   History of Linux 3
   Linux Distributions 3
Getting Started with Linux 5
   Installing Linux 5
   Choosing a Linux Distribution 6
   Dual Booting with Windows 8
Linux File System 10
   File Hierarchy Standard (FHS) 11
   File Permissions 13
   Navigating the File System 14
Command Line Basics 16
   Terminal Emulators 17
   Command Line Interface (CLI) 19
   Common Command Line Commands 20
Users and Groups 23
   Creating User Accounts: 24
   User Management Commands 25
   Group Management Commands 27
Package Management 29
   Software Repositories 30
   Package Managers 32
   Installing and Updating Software 33
Linux Shell and Shell Scripting 35

Shell Types (Bash, Zsh, etc.).................................36
Shell Variables... 38
Writing and Running Shell Scripts............................ 39
Writing and Running Shell Scripts........................ 42
Working with Files and Directories........................... 45
Text Processing Tools: grep, sed, awk........................ 46
Networking in Linux.......................................48
IP Addressing and Subnetting.................................50
Common Network Utilities.....................................52
System Monitoring and Maintenance........................ 54
Process Management... 55
Log Files and System Logging................................. 58
Troubleshooting and Debugging............................ 61
Common Linux Issues.. 63
Diagnosing and Fixing Problems...............................65
Useful Troubleshooting Tools.................................67
conclusion...69

Chapter one

Introduction to Linux

What is Linux?

Linux is an open-source operating system that was initially developed by Linus Torvalds in 1991. It is built on the Unix operating system and is known for its stability, security, and flexibility.

Linux is based on the Linux kernel, which serves as the core of the operating system. It provides the essential functions and interfaces required for other software components to run on top of it.

History of Linux

Linux has its roots in the Unix operating system, which was developed in the 1970s. Unix became popular in academic and research institutions due to its powerful features and multi-user capabilities.

In 1991, Linus Torvalds, a Finnish computer science student, created the Linux kernel as a hobby project. He shared it with the online community and invited collaboration and improvement from others.

Over time, developers worldwide contributed to the Linux kernel and created various distributions (or "distros") that packaged the Linux kernel with additional software and tools, making it more accessible and user-friendly.

Linux Distributions

A Linux distribution, or distro, refers to a complete operating system built around the Linux kernel. It includes the kernel itself, along with a collection of software packages, libraries, and utilities.

Popular Linux distributions include Ubuntu, Fedora, Debian, CentOS, and Linux Mint. Each distribution has its own characteristics, target audience, and package management system.

Distributions often come with a desktop environment, which provides a graphical user interface (GUI) and various applications for easy interaction with the operating system.

Advantages of Linux

Open-source: Linux is distributed under open-source licences, allowing users to view, modify, and distribute the source code. This fosters a collaborative development community and encourages innovation.

Stability and Security: Linux is known for its stability and security features. It is less prone to crashes, malware, and other security vulnerabilities compared to other operating systems.

Customization: Linux provides a high degree of customization. Users can choose from a wide range of desktop environments, themes, and software packages to create a personalised computing experience.

Command Line Interface (CLI): Linux offers a powerful command-line interface, allowing users to perform complex tasks efficiently through text commands.

Compatibility: Linux can run on various hardware architectures, from desktop computers to servers and embedded systems. It also supports a wide range of software applications.

Uses of Linux

Server Systems: Linux is widely used for hosting web servers, database servers, file servers, and other types of server systems due to its stability, security, and performance.

Desktop Computing: Linux desktop distributions provide an alternative to Windows and macOS, offering a free and customizable operating system with a range of software applications.

Embedded Systems: Linux is extensively used in embedded systems such as smartphones, tablets, smart TVs, routers, and IoT devices due to its flexibility, scalability, and low resource requirements.

Scientific and Academic Research: Linux is favoured in scientific and academic environments for its availability of powerful tools and software packages used in data analysis, simulation, and research.

Overall, Linux is a versatile and robust operating system that has gained popularity due to its open-source nature, stability, security, and flexibility. Whether you're a newcomer or an experienced user, understanding the fundamental concepts of Linux is essential to harness its power and make the most out of this operating system.

Chapter 2

Getting Started with Linux

Installing Linux

Before getting started with Linux, you'll need to install it on your computer. Most Linux distributions provide installation media that can be downloaded from their official websites.

The installation process may vary slightly depending on the distribution you choose. Generally, you'll need to create a bootable USB or DVD from the downloaded ISO file and follow the on-screen instructions to install Linux on your system.

During installation, you'll have the option to choose the installation type, partition the hard drive, and select additional software packages to install. It's recommended to allocate separate partitions for the root directory ("/") and the home directory ("/home") to keep your personal files separate from the system files.

Choosing a Linux Distribution

Linux offers a wide range of distributions, each with its own strengths and characteristics. The choice of distribution depends on your requirements, preferences, and level of expertise.

Ubuntu is a popular beginner-friendly distribution known for its user-friendly interface and extensive community support. Other distributions like Fedora, Debian, and Linux Mint also provide user-friendly environments and come with pre-installed software.

If you prefer a more minimalistic approach or want to customise your Linux experience extensively, you might consider distributions like Arch Linux or Gentoo. These distributions require more technical knowledge but provide greater flexibility and control.

Dual Booting with Windows

If you're already using Windows on your computer and want to keep it alongside Linux, you can set up a dual-boot configuration.

First, create a separate partition for Linux on your hard drive. This can be done during the Linux installation process or by using a partitioning tool like GParted before installing Linux.

Install Linux on the created partition, ensuring you choose the correct partition during the installation process.

Once Linux is installed, you'll have the option to choose between Linux and Windows during the system startup, allowing you to select the desired operating system each time you boot your computer.

Navigating the Linux File System

Linux follows a hierarchical file system structure known as the File Hierarchy Standard (FHS). Understanding the basic structure will help you navigate and work with files and directories in Linux.

The root directory ("/") is the top-level directory and contains all other directories and files.

Common directories include:

/home: User home directories.

/etc: Configuration files.

/bin: Essential system binaries.

/usr: User-installed programs and libraries.

/var: Variable data, such as log files and temporary files.

/tmp: Temporary files.

The "cd" command is used to change directories, "ls" to list files and directories, "pwd" to display the current directory, and "mkdir" to create directories.

Graphical User Interface (GUI) and Desktop Environments

Linux distributions typically provide a graphical user interface (GUI) that allows you to interact with the operating system using windows, icons, menus, and other visual elements.

The GUI is often provided by a desktop environment, such as GNOME, KDE, Xfce, or Cinnamon. Each desktop environment has its own look, feel, and set of default applications.

To launch applications in the GUI, you can use the application launcher or search for specific applications. You can also customise the desktop environment by changing themes, wallpapers, and other settings.

Getting started with Linux may seem overwhelming at first, but with the right distribution and a basic understanding of the installation process, file system navigation, and desktop environment, you'll be on your way to exploring and harnessing the power of Linux. As you gain more experience, you can delve into advanced topics, such as command-line usage, system administration, and software customization.

Choosing a Linux Distribution

When starting your Linux journey, one of the first decisions you'll need to make is selecting a Linux distribution. With numerous options available, it's important to choose a distribution that aligns with your needs, preferences, and level of expertise. Here are some factors to consider when choosing a Linux distribution:

User-Friendliness: If you're new to Linux or prefer a user-friendly experience, distributions like Ubuntu, Linux Mint, Fedora, and openSUSE are excellent choices. They provide intuitive graphical interfaces, easy-to-use software managers, and extensive documentation and community support for beginners.

Hardware Compatibility: Different Linux distributions may have varying levels of compatibility with hardware devices. Before choosing a distribution, check if it supports your hardware components such as graphics cards, Wi-Fi adapters, printers, and other peripherals. Distributions like Ubuntu and Fedora often have good hardware compatibility due to their wide user base and active development communities.

Desktop Environment: Linux distributions offer different desktop environments, each with its own visual style, functionality, and resource requirements. The most popular desktop environments include GNOME, KDE Plasma, Xfce, and Cinnamon. Take some time to explore the different desktop environments and choose the one that suits your workflow and aesthetic preferences.

Software Availability: Consider the availability of software packages in the distribution's repositories. Most Linux distributions have vast repositories of software applications that can be easily installed with package managers. However, some distributions may have more extensive repositories than others. Ensure that the distribution you choose has the software you need for your intended use, such as productivity tools, multimedia applications, development environments, or specialised software for specific tasks.

Support and Community: The Linux community is known for its strong support and active participation. Some distributions have larger and more active communities, which means you'll have access to extensive online documentation, forums, and user groups for troubleshooting, learning, and seeking assistance. Ubuntu, for example, has a large and helpful community, making it an excellent choice for beginners.

Stability vs. Cutting Edge: Linux distributions range from stable, long-term support (LTS) releases to bleeding-edge distributions that provide the latest software versions. Stable distributions like Debian and CentOS prioritise stability and reliability, making them suitable for production servers or users who prefer a more conservative approach. On the other hand, distributions like Arch Linux and Fedora emphasise providing the latest software updates and features for users who want to stay at the forefront of technology.

Customizability: Linux is highly customizable, allowing you to tailor the operating system to your liking. If you enjoy tweaking and customising your system extensively, distributions like Arch Linux and Gentoo provide greater flexibility and control over the installation and configuration process. However, they require more technical expertise and a willingness to invest time in learning and maintaining the system.

Ultimately, the choice of a Linux distribution depends on your specific needs, preferences, and level of expertise. It's worth trying out different distributions by creating live USBs or running them in virtual machines to get a feel for their user interfaces and functionalities. Remember that you can always switch distributions or have multiple distributions installed in a dual-boot configuration to explore different options and find the one that suits you best.

Dual Booting with Windows

If you're already using Windows on your computer and want to try out Linux without completely replacing your existing operating system, dual booting is a great option. Dual booting allows you to have both Windows and Linux installed on your machine, giving you the flexibility to choose the desired operating system at startup. Here's a step-by-step guide to dual booting Windows and Linux:

Backup Your Data: Before making any changes to your system, it's crucial to back up your important data. While the dual booting process is generally safe, it's always better to be prepared for any unforeseen circumstances.

Partition Your Hard Drive: You'll need to create a separate partition on your hard drive to install Linux. This partition will serve as the space for your Linux installation and will not affect your existing Windows installation. Windows provides a built-in partitioning tool called Disk Management, or you can use third-party tools like GParted to resize your Windows partition and create a new partition for Linux.

Choose a Linux Distribution: Select the Linux distribution you want to install. Consider factors such as user-friendliness, hardware compatibility, software availability, and community support. Popular beginner-friendly distributions include Ubuntu, Linux Mint, and Fedora.

Create Bootable Media: Download the ISO file for your chosen Linux distribution and create a bootable USB or DVD. Various tools like Rufus, BalenaEtcher, or UNetbootin can help you create a bootable USB.

Disable Secure Boot: If your computer has Secure Boot enabled, you might need to disable it in the BIOS/UEFI settings. Secure Boot is a security feature that verifies the authenticity of the operating system during the boot process. Some Linux distributions may not have the necessary digital signatures to work with Secure Boot enabled, so it's often easier to disable it before installation.

Install Linux: Insert the bootable media into your computer and restart it. Follow the installation wizard of your chosen Linux distribution. When prompted for the installation type, choose the option for custom or manual partitioning. Select the partition you created earlier for Linux and assign it as the root ("/") partition. Make sure not to format or touch your Windows partition.

Install the Boot Loader: During the Linux installation process, you'll be prompted to install a boot loader. Choose to install it on the same hard drive where your Windows installation is located. The boot loader (usually GRUB) will allow you to choose between Windows and Linux at startup.

Complete the Installation: Follow the remaining steps of the installation process, including creating a user account and configuring additional settings. Once the installation is complete, reboot your computer.

Choose Your Operating System: After rebooting, you'll see a boot menu where you can select the operating system you want to use. Use the arrow keys to highlight your desired option (Windows or Linux) and press Enter to boot into the selected operating system.

Congratulations! You have successfully set up a dual-boot configuration with Windows and Linux on your computer.

Now, whenever you start your computer, you'll have the option to choose between Windows and Linux.

Note: It's essential to keep both your Windows and Linux installations updated with the latest security patches and updates. Be cautious when modifying partitions or changing system settings to avoid accidental data loss or system instability.

Chapter three

Linux File System

The Linux operating system follows a hierarchical file system structure, which is similar to the Unix file system. Understanding the Linux file system is essential for navigating and managing files and directories effectively. Here are the key components of the Linux file system:

Root Directory ("/"): The root directory is the top-level directory in the file system hierarchy. It serves as the starting point for all file paths in Linux. The root directory is represented by a forward slash ("/").

Directories (Folders): Directories, also known as folders, are used to organise files in a hierarchical manner. They can contain both files and other directories. Directories in Linux are case-sensitive.

Files: Files in Linux can be categorised into various types, such as text files, executable files, configuration files, and more. Files are stored within directories and are identified by their names.

File Paths: A file path is the unique address or location of a file within the file system hierarchy. It consists of a series of directory names separated by slashes ("/"). For example,

"/home/user/Documents/myfile.txt" is a file path that points to the file named "myfile.txt" located in the "Documents" directory within the "user" directory, which is in the "home" directory.

Common Directories:
/bin: This directory contains essential system binaries (executable files) that are required for basic system functionality. These binaries are accessible to all users.
/boot: The boot directory contains files related to the system boot process, such as the kernel, initial RAM disk (initrd), and boot loader configuration files.
/etc: Configuration files for system-wide settings and applications are stored in this directory. It includes files for network configuration, user authentication, software repositories, and more.
/home: Each user on a Linux system has a separate directory under /home, where their personal files and settings are stored. For example, /home/user is the home directory for the user named "user."
/root: The root user's home directory is located at /root. This directory is typically only accessible to the root user and contains configuration files specific to the root user.
/tmp: The tmp directory is used for temporary files that are created and used by various applications. Files in this directory are typically deleted upon system reboot.
/var: This directory contains variable data, such as log files, spool files, and temporary files generated by system processes or applications.

Command Line Operations:

The "cd" command is used to change directories. For example, "cd /home/user" changes the current directory to /home/user.

The "ls" command lists files and directories in the current directory. Additional options like "-l" (long format) and "-a" (including hidden files) can be used for more detailed listings.

The "pwd" command displays the current working directory (i.e., the directory you are currently in).

The "mkdir" command is used to create directories. For example, "mkdir mydir" creates a directory named "mydir" in the current directory.

Understanding the Linux file system structure and the various directories it contains is crucial for efficiently managing and organising files and directories. By using commands like "cd," "ls," "pwd," and "mkdir," you can navigate, list, locate, and create directories and files within the Linux file system.

File Hierarchy Standard (FHS)

The File Hierarchy Standard (FHS) is a set of guidelines that define the directory structure and organisation of files in Unix-like operating systems, including Linux. The FHS aims to provide consistency across different distributions and facilitate software interoperability. Understanding the key directories defined by the FHS can help users navigate and manage files effectively. Here are the main directories defined by the FHS:

/bin: This directory contains essential system binaries (executable files) that are required for basic system functionality. These binaries are accessible to all users and typically include common commands like ls, cp, rm, and mkdir.

/boot: The /boot directory contains files related to the system boot process. This includes the kernel, initial RAM disk (initrd), boot loader configuration files (such as GRUB), and other files necessary for booting the system.

/dev: The /dev directory contains device files that represent various devices connected to the system, such as hard drives, input/output devices, and terminals. These device files provide a way for programs to interact with hardware devices.

/etc: Configuration files for system-wide settings and applications are stored in the /etc directory. It includes files for network configuration (e.g., /etc/network/interfaces), user authentication (e.g., /etc/passwd, /etc/group), software repositories (e.g., /etc/apt/sources.list), and more.

/home: Each user on a Linux system has a separate directory under /home, where their personal files and settings are stored. For example, /home/user is the home directory for the user named "user." User-specific configuration files and data are typically stored in subdirectories within their respective home directories.

/lib and /lib64: These directories contain shared libraries required by programs and system utilities. The /lib directory contains libraries for 32-bit systems, while /lib64 (or /lib/x86_64-linux-gnu) contains libraries for 64-bit systems.

/media and /mnt: The /media directory is used for mounting removable media devices such as USB drives, CDs, and DVDs. On the other hand, the /mnt directory is a generic mount point for temporarily mounting file systems. It is often used for manually mounting external or network file systems.

/opt: The /opt directory is intended for installing optional (hence the name) third-party software packages. It provides a location for self-contained software installations that are not part of the core system distribution.

/sbin: The /sbin directory contains system binaries that are primarily used by system administrators for system maintenance and management tasks. These binaries typically require administrative privileges to run and include utilities like fsck, ifconfig, and iptables.

/tmp: The /tmp directory is used for storing temporary files created by various applications and processes. Files in this directory are typically deleted upon system reboot, although the distribution-specific policies may vary.

/usr: The /usr directory contains user-installed programs, libraries, documentation, and other read-only data for general system use. It is further organised into subdirectories, such as /usr/bin for user binaries, /usr/lib for libraries, /usr/share for shared data, and /usr/include for C header files.

/var: The /var directory holds variable data that changes during system operation. This includes log files (/var/log), spool files (/var/spool), temporary files (/var/tmp), and other variable data generated by system processes and applications.

These are some of the key directories defined by the File Hierarchy Standard (FHS) in Linux. Adhering to this standard ensures consistency and ease of use across different Linux distributions, making it easier for software developers and system administrators to write portable and compatible code.

File Permissions

In Linux, file permissions are a crucial aspect of security and access control. They determine who can read, write, or execute files and directories. Understanding file permissions is essential for managing file access and protecting sensitive data. Here's a breakdown of Linux file permissions:

Permission Types:
Read (r): Allows a user to view the contents of a file or list the contents of a directory.
Write (w): Enables a user to modify a file or add/remove files within a directory.
Execute (x): Grants permission to execute a file (if it is a program or script) or access a directory.

Permission Classes:
Owner: The user who owns the file or directory.
Group: A group of users who share common permissions.
Others: Any other users who are not the owner or part of the group.

Symbolic Notation:
Each permission class is represented by three characters: "r" for read, "w" for write, and "x" for execute.
For example, "rwx" represents read, write, and execute permissions for a specific class.

A dash ("-") indicates the absence of a particular permission for a specific class.

Numeric Notation:
Each permission is assigned a numeric value: 4 for read, 2 for write, and 1 for execute.
The sum of these values represents the permission set for a specific class.
For example, "rwx" translates to 7 (4 + 2 + 1), "rw-" translates to 6 (4 + 2), and "r-x" translates to 5 (4 + 1)

File Permission Examples:
"-rw-r--r--": The owner has read and write permissions, while the group and others have read-only permissions.
"drwxr-xr-x": Represents a directory. The owner has read, write, and execute permissions, while the group and others have read and execute permissions.

Changing File Permissions:
The "chmod" command is used to modify file permissions. The permission can be modified using symbolic notation (e.g., "chmod u+w file.txt" to add write permission for the owner) or numeric notation (e.g., "chmod 644 file.txt" to set permissions as "-rw-r--r--").
Ownership can be changed using the "chown" command, and group ownership can be changed using the "chgrp" command.

File Permission Levels:

User: The owner of the file or directory.
Group: The group assigned to the file or directory.
Others: All other users who are not the owner or part of the group.

Understanding and managing file permissions is crucial for maintaining system security and controlling access to sensitive files and directories. It allows you to grant appropriate permissions to users and groups while restricting access to unauthorised users. Properly managing file permissions helps protect confidential data and prevent unauthorised modifications or executions of critical system files.

Navigating the File System

Navigating the file system is a fundamental skill in Linux that allows users to locate, access, and manage files and directories. Understanding how to navigate efficiently can significantly improve productivity. Here are some key commands and techniques for navigating the Linux file system:

Present Working Directory (pwd):

The "pwd" command displays the absolute path of the current working directory. It helps you identify your current location within the file system.

List Files and Directories (ls):
The "ls" command lists the files and directories in the current directory. By default, it displays only the names of the files and directories. However, using options such as "-l" (long format) or "-a" (including hidden files) provides more detailed information.

Change Directory (cd):
The "cd" command is used to change the current working directory. It allows you to navigate to a specific directory. For example:

"cd /path/to/directory" changes the current directory to the specified absolute path.
"cd directory" changes the current directory to a subdirectory within the current directory.
"cd .." moves up one level to the parent directory.
Pathnames:
Pathnames are used to specify the location of files and directories within the file system. There are two types of pathnames:

Absolute Pathname: Starts with the root directory ("/") and specifies the complete path to a file or directory.

Relative Pathname: Specifies the path relative to the current working directory.

Tab Completion:

Tab completion is a convenient feature that allows you to automatically complete file and directory names while typing a command. Pressing the Tab key after entering a few characters will auto-complete the name or display a list of possible options if there are multiple matches.

Special Directories:

"~" (tilde) represents the current user's home directory. For example, "cd ~" changes to the home directory.

"." (dot) refers to the current directory.

".." (dot-dot) represents the parent directory.

Path Shortcuts:

"/" (forward slash) is the root directory and the highest level in the file system hierarchy.

"~user" represents the home directory of the specified user. For example, "~john" refers to John's home directory.

"." (dot) is the current directory.

".." (dot-dot) is the parent directory.

File and Directory Names:

Linux file systems are case-sensitive, so "file.txt" and "File.txt" are considered different files.

Filenames can contain special characters, such as spaces, but it's recommended to avoid using them to simplify command-line operations. If necessary, use quotes or escape characters () to handle special characters.

By mastering these navigation techniques and commands like "pwd," "ls," and "cd," you can efficiently move through the Linux file system, locate files and directories, and perform various operations. Practise regularly to enhance your familiarity with the file system structure and improve your productivity when working with files and directories in Linux.

Chapter four

Command Line Basics

The command line interface (CLI) in Linux provides a powerful way to interact with the operating system. By typing commands, users can perform a wide range of tasks, from file management to system configuration. Here are some command line basics to get you started:

Opening the Terminal:
To access the command line interface, you need to open the terminal. The terminal is a program that provides a text-based interface for entering commands. You can find the terminal application in the applications menu or use the keyboard shortcut (e.g., Ctrl+Alt+T).

Command Structure:
Most commands follow a similar structure:
command [options] [arguments]
Command: The actual command to execute.
Options: Additional flags or switches that modify the behaviour of the command.
Arguments: Any input required by the command, such as filenames or directories.

Command Execution:

After typing a command, press Enter to execute it. The command will run, and the output, if any, will be displayed in the terminal. Some commands may require administrative privileges, in which case you'll be prompted to enter your password.

Getting Help:
Linux provides built-in documentation for most commands. You can access it using the "man" command followed by the name of the command you want to learn about. For example, "man ls" displays the manual page for the "ls" command. The manual page provides detailed information on the command's usage, options, and examples.

Commonly Used Commands:
"ls": Lists files and directories in the current directory.
"cd": Changes the current working directory.
"pwd": Displays the absolute path of the current working directory.
"mkdir": Creates a new directory.
"rm": Removes files and directories.
"cp": Copies files and directories.
"mv": Moves or renames files and directories.
"cat": Displays the contents of a file.
"grep": Searches for specific text patterns within files.
"chmod": Changes the permissions of files and directories.
"sudo": Executes a command with administrative privileges.
Autocompletion:

The command line offers autocompletion, a useful feature that completes commands, filenames, and paths automatically. Pressing the Tab key will complete the partially typed command or display available options if there are multiple matches.

Command History:
The terminal keeps a history of previously entered commands. To access previous commands, you can use the up and down arrow keys. Pressing the up arrow key will cycle through previous commands, allowing you to reuse or modify them.

Exiting the Terminal:
To exit the terminal, you can use the "exit" command or press Ctrl+D.

These command line basics provide a foundation for using the terminal in Linux. By familiarising yourself with common commands and practising their usage, you can efficiently navigate and manage files, configure system settings, and perform various administrative tasks using the command line interface.

Terminal Emulators

A terminal emulator is a program that allows users to interact with a command line interface on their computer. It provides a graphical interface for accessing the command line, enabling users to execute commands, run programs, and perform various tasks. Here's an overview of terminal emulators and their features:

Functionality:
Terminal emulators provide a virtual terminal environment within a graphical user interface (GUI). They replicate the functionality of traditional physical terminals, allowing users to type commands and receive output.

Text-Based Interface:
Terminal emulators display text-based output, typically using a monospaced font. This allows for the efficient rendering of command line commands, responses, and other text-based content.

Multiple Terminal Sessions:
Terminal emulators often support multiple terminal sessions within a single window. This feature enables users to work with multiple command line sessions simultaneously, switching between them as needed.

Customization Options:

Terminal emulators offer various customization options to personalise the appearance and behaviour of the terminal. Users can modify settings such as font size, colour schemes, cursor style, and keyboard shortcuts to suit their preferences.

Copy and Paste:
Terminal emulators support copy and paste functionality, allowing users to select and copy text from the terminal output and paste it into other applications or vice versa.

Scrollback Buffer:
Terminal emulators maintain a scrollback buffer, which stores a history of previously displayed output. Users can scroll up to view earlier command output or scroll down to access the most recent output.

Tabbed Interface:
Many terminal emulators support a tabbed interface, enabling users to have multiple terminal sessions open in separate tab
 within a single window. This simplifies workflow management and organisation.

Split Panes:
Some advanced terminal emulators offer the ability to split the terminal window into multiple panes, each displaying a different session. This feature allows for efficient multitasking and simultaneous execution of commands.

Remote Access:
Terminal emulators can be used for remote access to other systems, such as SSH (Secure Shell) sessions. They allow users to connect to remote servers or machines and work with their command line interfaces as if they were locally present.

Popular Terminal Emulators:
GNOME Terminal: The default terminal emulator for the GNOME desktop environment.
Konsole: The default terminal emulator for the KDE desktop environment.
Terminator: A feature-rich terminal emulator with advanced capabilities like split panes and tabs.
iTerm2: A popular terminal emulator for macOS, offering extensive customization options.
PuTTY: A widely used terminal emulator for Windows, primarily used for SSH connections.
Terminal emulators are essential tools for developers, system administrators, and power users who rely on the command line interface for efficient and powerful control over their systems. By providing a user-friendly interface to the command line, terminal emulators enhance productivity and enable seamless interaction with the underlying operating system.

Command Line Interface (CLI)

The Command Line Interface (CLI) is a text-based interface in which users interact with a computer system by entering commands. It provides a powerful and efficient way to perform various tasks, manage files, configure settings, and automate operations. Here's an overview of the Command Line Interface:

Structure:
The CLI operates on a simple principle: users enter commands as text strings, and the computer responds by executing those commands. Each command consists of a command name, followed by optional arguments and options.

Advantages of the CLI:
Efficiency: Command line operations often require fewer keystrokes than their graphical counterparts, enabling faster execution of tasks.
Automation: Commands can be combined and automated using scripts, allowing for batch processing and complex operations.
Resource Efficiency: The CLI typically consumes fewer system resources compared to graphical user interfaces (GUIs), making it suitable for low-resource environments.

Flexibility: The CLI provides granular control and precise configuration options, empowering users to perform advanced system operations.

Command Syntax:
Commands in the CLI generally follow a specific syntax: command [options] [arguments]
Command: The name of the command to execute.
Options: Additional flags or switches that modify the behaviour of the command.
Arguments: Any input required by the command, such as filenames, directory paths, or search patterns.

Common Commands:
There are numerous commands available in the CLI, each serving a specific purpose. Here are some commonly used commands across different platforms:

File and Directory Operations: ls, cd, mkdir, rm, cp, mv
Text Manipulation: cat, grep, sed, awk
System Information: uname, df, top, ps
Package Management: apt-get (Debian-based systems), yum (RHEL-based systems), pacman (Arch Linux)
Network Configuration: ifconfig, ip, ping, traceroute
Command Completion:
Most CLI environments provide command completion, which allows users to type a partial command and then press the Tab key to automatically complete it. This feature saves time and reduces typing errors.

Command History:
The CLI maintains a history of previously entered commands. Users can navigate through the command history using the arrow keys, enabling quick access to previously executed commands.

Help and Documentation:
CLI systems usually offer built-in documentation for commands. Users can access it by typing "man" followed by the name of the command they want to learn about. Manual pages provide comprehensive information about command usage, options, and examples.

Remote Access:
The CLI is commonly used for remote access to systems, allowing users to manage and administer remote machines via secure protocols like SSH (Secure Shell). This enables system administrators to control servers and devices remotely.

The Command Line Interface is a powerful tool for advanced users and system administrators. While it may have a learning curve, mastering the CLI provides users with precise control, automation capabilities, and efficient management of computer systems. With practice and familiarity, users can become proficient in utilising the full potential of the CLI for various tasks and operations.

Common Command Line Commands

The command line interface (CLI) provides a wide range of commands that allow users to interact with the operating system, manage files, configure settings, and perform various tasks. Here are some common command line commands that you'll frequently encounter:

Navigation Commands:
"ls": Lists files and directories in the current directory.
"cd": Changes the current working directory.
"pwd": Displays the absolute path of the current working directory.

File and Directory Management:
"mkdir": Creates a new directory.
"rm": Removes files and directories.
"cp": Copies files and directories.
"mv": Moves or renames files and directories.
"cat": Displays the contents of a file.
"touch": Creates an empty file or updates the timestamp of an existing file.

Text Manipulation:
"grep": Searches for specific text patterns within files.
"sed": Stream editor for text manipulation.

"awk": Powerful text processing tool for extracting and manipulating data.

File Permissions:
"chmod": Changes the permissions of files and directories.
"chown": Changes the ownership of files and directories.
"chgrp": Changes the group ownership of files and directories.

System Information:
"uname": Displays system information like the kernel name, version, and machine architecture.
"df": Shows disk space usage for file systems.
"top": Displays real-time information about system resources and processes.
"ps": Lists currently running processes.

Package Management:
"apt-get" (Debian-based systems): Manages packages and software repositories.
"yum" (RHEL-based systems): Instals, updates, and removes packages.
"pacman" (Arch Linux): Manages packages on Arch Linux.

Network Commands:
"ping": Sends ICMP echo requests to a network host to check connectivity.
"ifconfig" or "ip": Displays network interface configuration information.

"netstat": Shows network connections, routing tables, and network statistics.
"ssh": Connects to a remote machine using the SSH protocol.

File Compression and Archiving:
"tar": Creates compressed or uncompressed archives.
"gzip" or "gunzip": Compresses or decompresses files.
"zip" or "unzip": Creates or extracts ZIP archives.

User and Group Management:
"useradd" and "userdel": Create and delete user accounts.
"passwd": Sets or changes user passwords.
"groupadd" and "groupdel": Create and delete groups.

System Administration:
"sudo": Executes a command with administrative privileges.
"reboot" and "shutdown": Restarts or shuts down the system.
"cron": Schedules recurring tasks or commands.

These are just a few examples of common command line commands. The command line offers a vast array of commands and utilities, allowing users to perform complex operations, automate tasks, and effectively manage their systems. By familiarising yourself with these commands and exploring their options and variations, you can become proficient in utilising the command line interface to its full potential.

Chapter five

Users and Groups

In a Linux-based operating system, users and groups are fundamental concepts that help manage access to system resources and provide a level of security. Understanding users and groups is essential for effective system administration. Here's an overview of users and groups in Linux:

Users:
User Accounts:
Each person who interacts with the system has a user account. User accounts provide a unique identity and a way to authenticate and authorise individuals.
Usernames are used to log in to the system and identify users.
User accounts store personal settings, files, and configurations specific to each user.

User IDs (UID):
User IDs are numeric identifiers assigned to each user account. They uniquely identify each user on the system. UID 0 is reserved for the superuser or root account, which has administrative privileges and can perform system-wide tasks

Passwords and Authentication:
User accounts are protected by passwords or other authentication mechanisms to ensure only authorised users can access the system.
Users can change their passwords and reset them if forgotten.

User Home Directory:
Each user has a home directory, which serves as their default location upon login.
Home directories store personal files and configurations for each user.

Groups:
Group Accounts:
Groups are collections of user accounts with similar access permissions and privileges.
Group accounts simplify access control and file sharing by granting permissions to a group rather than individual users.

Group IDs (GID):
Group IDs are numeric identifiers assigned to each group. They uniquely identify each group on the system.

Primary and Secondary Groups:
Each user account has a primary group associated with it, which is the default group for file ownership and access.

Users can also be members of multiple secondary groups, allowing them to share resources with other group members.

Group Permissions:
File permissions can be set for users, groups, and others. Group permissions allow fine-grained control over access to files and directories by members of a particular group.

System Administration:
Creating and Managing Users:
Administrators can create new user accounts, modify account settings, and delete accounts.
Useradd and userdel are common commands for adding and removing user accounts.

Creating and Managing Groups:
Administrators can create groups, modify group settings, and delete groups.
Groupadd and groupdel are common commands for adding and removing groups.

Granting and Revoking Privileges:
Administrators can assign users to specific groups to grant them access privileges.
By using the appropriate file permissions, administrators can control read, write, and execute permissions for users and groups.

Managing users and groups is crucial for maintaining a secure and well-organised Linux system. By assigning appropriate access rights and permissions, administrators can ensure that resources are accessible to authorised users while protecting sensitive data. Understanding the concepts of users and groups is fundamental to effective system administration and access control.

Creating User Accounts:

Administrators can create new user accounts using the "useradd" command or graphical tools provided by the distribution.

During the account creation process, administrators set the username, password, user ID, home directory, and other account-specific settings.

Modifying User Accounts:
Administrators can modify user account settings such as the password, home directory, shell, and other attributes using commands like "usermod" or graphical tools.

Deleting User Accounts:

Administrators can remove user accounts using the "userdel" command. When an account is deleted, its associated files and settings are usually removed as well.

User Account Management:
System administrators are responsible for managing user accounts, ensuring that appropriate access rights and permissions are granted to each user.
Regular monitoring and periodic review of user accounts can help maintain the security and integrity of the system. Managing user accounts effectively is essential for maintaining a secure and organised Linux system. By assigning appropriate access rights, enforcing password policies, and reviewing user privileges, system administrators can ensure that resources are accessible to authorised users while protecting sensitive data. User accounts form the basis of user management and access control in Linux systems.

User Management Commands

In a Linux-based operating system, user management commands allow system administrators to create, modify, and delete user accounts, as well as perform various administrative tasks related to user management. These commands provide powerful capabilities for managing user accounts efficiently. Here are some commonly used user management commands in Linux:

1. useradd:
   - The "useradd" command is used to create a new user account.
   - Syntax: useradd [options] username
   - Example: useradd john

2. usermod:
   - The "usermod" command is used to modify user account settings.
   - Syntax: usermod [options] username
   - Example: usermod -s /bin/zsh john

3. userdel:
   - The "userdel" command is used to delete a user account.
   - Syntax: userdel [options] username
   - Example: userdel -r john (the "-r" option removes the user's home directory and mail spool)

4. passwd:
   - The "passwd" command is used to set or change a user's password.
   - Syntax: passwd [options] username
   - Example: passwd john

5. chage:
   - The "chage" command is used to modify user password expiration settings.

- Syntax: chage [options] username
- Example: chage -M 90 john (sets the maximum password age to 90 days)

6. su:
    - The "su" command is used to switch to another user account.
    - Syntax: su [options] [username]
    - Example: su - john (switches to the user account "john")

7. sudo:
    - The "sudo" command allows users to execute commands with administrative privileges.
    - Syntax: sudo [command]
    - Example: sudo apt update (runs the "apt update" command with administrative privileges)

8. finger:
    - The "finger" command provides detailed information about a user account, including the user's full name, home directory, and login status.
    - Syntax: finger [options] [username]
    - Example: finger john

9. w:

- The "w" command displays information about currently logged-in users and their activities.
- Syntax: w [options]
- Example: w

These commands provide essential functionality for user management in a Linux system. System administrators can use them to create and delete user accounts, modify user settings, set passwords, and perform administrative tasks. Understanding and effectively using these user management commands enables administrators to maintain a secure and well-managed user environment in a Linux system.

Group Management Commands

In a Linux-based operating system, group management commands allow system administrators to create, modify, and delete groups, as well as perform various administrative tasks related to group management. These commands provide powerful capabilities for managing groups efficiently. Here are some commonly used group management commands in Linux:

groupadd:
The "groupadd" command is used to create a new group.
Syntax: groupadd [options] group name
Example: groupadd developers

groupmod:
The "groupmod" command is used to modify group settings.
Syntax: groupmod [options] group name
Example: groupmod -g 1001 developers (changes the GID of the "developers" group to 1001)

groupdel:
The "groupdel" command is used to delete a group.
Syntax: groupdel groupname
Example: groupdel developers

usermod:
The "usermod" command is also used for group management tasks.
Syntax: usermod [options] username
Example: usermod -G developers john (adds the user "john" to the "developers" group)

groups:
The "groups" command displays the groups a user belongs to.
Syntax: groups [username]

Example: groups john

id:
The "id" command displays the group ID (GID) of a user or group.
Syntax: id [options] [username|groupname]
Example: id developers

getent:
The "getent" command retrieves entries from the system's databases, including groups.
Syntax: getent [database] [key]
Example: getent group developers

newgrp:
The "newgrp" command allows users to switch to another group temporarily.
Syntax: newgrp [group name]
Example: newgrp developers (switches to the "developers" group)

chgrp:
The "chgrp" command changes the group ownership of files and directories.
Syntax: chgrp [options] groupname file
Example: chgrp developers myfile.txt (assigns the "developers" group as the group owner of "myfile.txt")

gpasswd:

The "gpasswd" command is used for managing group passwords and membership.

Syntax: gpasswd [options] group name

Example: gpasswd -a john developers (adds the user "john" to the "developers" group)

These group management commands provide essential functionality for managing groups in a Linux system. System administrators can use them to create and delete groups, modify group settings, manage group membership, and assign group ownership to files and directories. Understanding and effectively using these group management commands enables administrators to maintain a well-organised and secure user environment in a Linux system.

Chapter six

Package Management

Package management is a vital aspect of Linux-based operating systems that simplifies the installation, upgrading, and removal of software packages. It provides a convenient and centralised method for managing software on a system. Package managers handle dependencies, resolve conflicts, and ensure the stability and security of the software ecosystem. Here's an overview of package management in Linux:

Package Manager:
A package manager is a software tool that automates the process of installing, updating, and removing software packages.
Different Linux distributions use different package managers. Some common package managers include:
APT (Advanced Package Tool): Used in Debian-based distributions like Ubuntu.
YUM (Yellowdog Updater Modified): Used in Red Hat-based distributions like Fedora and CentOS.
DNF (Dandified YUM): A newer package manager, replacing YUM in newer versions of Fedora.
Pacman: Used in Arch Linux and its derivatives.
Zypper: Used in SUSE Linux.

Package managers provide a command-line interface and often have graphical frontends for user-friendly package management.

Package Repository:

Package managers access software packages from online repositories, which are centralised software collections. Repositories contain pre-compiled software packages, along with metadata such as package descriptions, version numbers, and dependencies.
Each distribution has its official repositories, which are maintained and curated by the distribution's developers. Additional third-party repositories can be added to access a wider range of software.

Package Operations:

Package managers can perform various operations on software packages, including:
Installation: Instals software packages and their dependencies.
Upgrade: Updates installed packages to newer versions.
Removal: Uninstalls software packages and their associated files.
Search: Searches for packages based on specified criteria, such as package name or description.
Dependency Resolution: Automatically handles dependencies required by packages, ensuring that all necessary components are installed.

Repository Management: Enables the addition, removal, and configuration of software repositories.

Package Formats:
Packages are typically distributed in specific formats that are compatible with the respective package manager.
Examples of package formats include:
Debian Packages (.deb): Used in Debian-based distributions like Ubuntu.
RPM Packages (.rpm): Used in Red Hat-based distributions like Fedora and CentOS.
Arch Linux Packages (.pkg.tar.zst): Used in Arch Linux and its derivatives.
Tarballs (.tar.gz or .tar.bz2): Contain source code, which needs to be compiled and installed manually

System Updates:
Package managers also handle system updates, including security patches, bug fixes, and new features.
By regularly updating the system, users ensure they have the latest software versions with critical fixes and improvements.
Package management is a critical component of Linux systems, simplifying the software installation and maintenance process. It provides a centralised and efficient method for managing software packages, ensuring system stability, security, and ease of use. With package management, users can easily discover, install, update, and remove software, enhancing their overall Linux experience.

Software Repositories

In Linux-based operating systems, software repositories are centralised collections of software packages that are managed and maintained by the distribution's developers or third-party contributors. Repositories provide a convenient and secure way to access a wide range of software, ensuring easy installation, updates, and removal of applications. Here's an overview of software repositories in Linux:

Official Repositories:
Official repositories are the primary software sources provided by the distribution's developers.
These repositories contain a curated selection of software packages that are tested and approved for use on the specific distribution.
Official repositories are typically divided into different sections, such as the main, universe, multiverse, and restricted sections in Ubuntu.

Third-Party Repositories:
Third-party repositories are additional software sources created and maintained by individuals, organisations, or communities.

These repositories provide access to software packages that may not be available in the official repositories or offer alternative versions of existing packages.

Third-party repositories are often used to access bleeding-edge software, specialised applications, or proprietary software.

Repository Management:
The package manager of a Linux distribution is responsible for managing repositories.

Users can add or remove repositories, enable or disable them, and prioritise the order in which repositories are consulted during package installations and updates.

Repository management tools, such as apt, yum, dnf, zypper, or pacman, provide command-line interfaces and graphical frontends for repository management.

Mirrors:
Repositories are often mirrored across multiple servers located in different geographical locations.

Mirrors help distribute the load and improve download speeds for users.

Users can select a preferred mirror to download packages from or allow the package manager to automatically choose the fastest mirror.

Package Signing:
To ensure the authenticity and integrity of software packages, repositories often use digital signatures.

Packages are signed by the repository's maintainers using cryptographic keys.

The package manager verifies the package's signature before installation to prevent the installation of tampered or malicious software.

Updates and Security Patches:
Software repositories regularly provide updates, including security patches, bug fixes, and new features.

System administrators and users are encouraged to keep their systems up to date to ensure they have the latest software versions with critical fixes and improvements.

Package Repository Tools:
Besides the package manager, additional tools are available to manage repositories effectively.

For example, apt-get and aptitude are commonly used alongside APT-based package managers for advanced repository operations.

Managing software repositories is essential for obtaining a wide range of software and keeping Linux systems up to date. By leveraging official repositories and carefully selected third-party repositories, users can access an extensive catalogue of software packages while maintaining system stability, security, and compatibility. Software repositories contribute to the flexibility and versatility of Linux systems, allowing users to customise their software environment to suit their needs.

Package Managers

In Linux-based operating systems, package managers are software tools that automate the management of software packages. They provide a convenient and centralised way to install, update, and remove software, handle dependencies, and ensure the stability and security of the system. Here's an overview of package managers in Linux:

APT (Advanced Package Tool):
APT is the package manager used in Debian-based distributions like Ubuntu.
APT uses the .deb package format and operates with repositories containing pre-compiled packages.
APT provides command-line tools like apt-get and apt, as well as graphical front ends like Synaptic and GNOME Software.

YUM (Yellowdog Updater Modified) and DNF (Dandified YUM):
YUM was the package manager initially used in Red Hat-based distributions like Fedora and CentOS.
In newer versions of Fedora, YUM has been replaced by DNF, which is a redesigned and improved package manager.
Both YUM and DNF use the .rpm package format and work with repositories.

Command-line tools include yum and dnf, with graphical frontends like DNFdragora and GNOME Software.

Pacman:
Pacman is the package manager used in Arch Linux and its derivatives.
Pacman uses the .pkg.tar.zst package format and operates with the rolling-release model.
It features a simple command-line interface, with utilities like pacman, yaourt, and pamac for package management.

Zypper:
Zypper is the package manager used in SUSE Linux and openSUSE distributions.
Zypper uses the .rpm package format and works with repositories.
It offers a command-line interface for package management tasks.

Portage:
Portage is the package manager used in Gentoo Linux.
Portage uses the concept of source-based package management, where packages are compiled from source code.
Portage provides a flexible and customizable command-line interface for managing software.

Snap and Flatpak:

Snap and Flatpak are universal package formats and package management systems designed to work across different Linux distributions.

They bundle software packages with their dependencies, allowing for easier distribution and installation.

Snap packages are managed by the Snapd daemon and can be installed using the snap command.

Flatpak packages are managed by the Flatpak runtime and can be installed using the flatpak command.

These are just a few examples of package managers used in various Linux distributions. Each package manager has its own set of commands, options, and capabilities, but they all serve the purpose of simplifying software management.

Package managers ensure that software installations are efficient, updates are easy to apply, and dependencies are automatically resolved. They play a crucial role in maintaining a well-organised and up-to-date software environment on Linux systems.

Installing and Updating Software

In Linux-based operating systems, installing and updating software is made simple and efficient through the use of package managers. Package managers automate the process of retrieving, installing, and updating software packages, ensuring that users have access to the latest versions of their desired applications. Here's an overview of how to install and update software using package managers:

Installing Software:
To install software using a package manager, open a terminal or package manager GUI and use the appropriate command for your distribution.
For example, with APT (used in Debian-based distributions), you can use the command sudo apt-get install package_name to install a package.
Similarly, with YUM (used in Red Hat-based distributions), you can use the command sudo yum install package_name.
If you're using DNF (the successor to YUM), the command would be sudo dnf install package_name.
For Pacman (used in Arch Linux), you can use the command sudo pacman -S package_name.
The package manager will handle the retrieval and installation of the specified package, along with any required dependencies.

Updating Software:
Regularly updating software is crucial for security fixes, bug patches, and feature enhancements.
To update software using a package manager, run the appropriate command for your distribution.

For APT, you can use the command sudo apt-get update to refresh the package lists, followed by sudo apt-get upgrade to update the installed packages.

With YUM or DNF, you can use the command sudo yum update or sudo dnf update respectively to update the installed packages.

For Pacman, the command is sudo pacman -Syu to synchronise package databases and upgrade all installed packages.

Managing Software Repositories:

Software repositories act as centralised sources of software packages.

Package managers typically manage repositories automatically, but users can customise and manage repositories manually if needed.

You can add, remove, enable, or disable repositories through configuration files or dedicated repository management tools.

Consult the documentation or community resources specific to your distribution for detailed instructions on managing repositories.

Graphical Frontends:

Many package managers have graphical frontends that provide a user-friendly interface for installing and updating software.

These frontends, such as Synaptic, GNOME Software, or Discover, allow users to search for packages, browse categories, and handle installations and updates through a graphical interface.

Additional Package Formats:
In addition to using package managers, you may encounter other package formats like Snap, Flatpak, or AppImage. These package formats provide a way to distribute software independently of the distribution's package manager and can be installed alongside traditional packages.
The installation process for these formats may differ from the standard package manager commands, so consult the respective documentation for installation and update instructions.
By leveraging the power of package managers, users can easily install, update, and manage software packages on their Linux systems. Package managers simplify the process, handle dependencies, and ensure a consistent and secure software environment. Regularly updating software keeps the system up to date with the latest features, bug fixes, and security patches, enhancing the overall user experience.

Chapter seven

Linux Shell and Shell Scripting

In Linux-based operating systems, the shell serves as the command-line interpreter and interface between the user and the operating system. The shell allows users to interact with the system, run commands, and execute shell scripts to automate tasks. Here's an overview of the Linux shell and shell scripting:

Shell:
The shell is a program that interprets user commands and executes them.
Commonly used shells in Linux include:
Bash (Bourne Again SHell): The default shell for most Linux distributions.
Zsh (Z Shell): An extended and customizable shell with additional features.
Fish (Friendly Interactive SHell): A user-friendly shell with interactive autocompletion and syntax highlighting.
The shell provides a command-line interface (CLI) where users can enter commands and receive output.

Shell Prompt:

The shell prompt is displayed in the terminal to indicate that the shell is ready to accept commands.
The prompt usually includes information like the username, hostname, current working directory, and other details.
The prompt can be customised to meet personal preferences or display additional information.

Shell Commands:
Shell commands are instructions given to the shell to perform specific tasks.
Linux provides a wide range of commands for various purposes, including file manipulation, process management, networking, and system administration.
Commands can be entered directly in the shell or executed from shell scripts.

Shell Scripting:
Shell scripting involves writing scripts that contain a series of shell commands to automate tasks.
Shell scripts are plain text files with executable permissions that can be run as programs.
Shell scripts can include variables, conditional statements, loops, and other programming constructs to create complex workflows and automation.
Shell scripts are often used for system administration, automation, and repetitive tasks.

Script Execution:

To execute a shell script, it must have executable permissions. This can be done using the chmod command. Shell scripts can be executed by specifying the script file's path or by making it executable and running it directly, like ./script.sh.
Shell scripts can take arguments passed from the command line and use them within the script.

Shebang (#!):
The shebang is a special line at the beginning of a shell script that specifies the interpreter to be used to execute the script.
For example, #!/bin/bash indicates that the script should be run using the Bash shell.
The shebang line allows the script to be executed directly, without explicitly specifying the interpreter on the command line.

Environment Variables:
Environment variables are dynamic values that the system and processes use to configure behaviour or provide information.
Linux provides various predefined environment variables that can be accessed and modified within shell scripts.
Users can also define custom environment variables for their specific needs.
Shell scripting in Linux offers immense power and flexibility, allowing users to automate repetitive tasks, customise their workflows, and create complex system

administration routines. By leveraging the shell's capabilities and understanding the syntax and features of shell scripting, users can enhance productivity and efficiently manage their Linux systems.

Shell Types (Bash, Zsh, etc.)

In Linux and Unix-based operating systems, different shell types are available, each offering its own features, customization options, and interactive capabilities. Let's explore some of the commonly used shell types:

Bash (Bourne Again SHell):
Bash is the most widely used shell and the default shell in most Linux distributions.
It is an extended version of the original Bourne shell (sh) and includes additional features and enhancements.
Bash supports command-line editing, history, tab completion, and job control, making it user-friendly and efficient.
Many shell scripts and system administration tasks are written specifically for Bash.

Zsh (Z Shell):

Zsh is a highly customizable shell known for its extended features and interactive capabilities.

It offers advanced tab completion, spelling correction, syntax highlighting, and advanced customization options.

Zsh includes powerful globbing patterns and supports plugins and themes to enhance the user experience.

With its extensibility and rich set of features, Zsh is popular among power users and developers.

Fish (Friendly Interactive SHell):
Fish is designed to be a user-friendly and intuitive shell with a focus on interactive usage.

It features interactive autocompletion, syntax highlighting, and a consistent and readable command syntax.

Fish emphasises simplicity and discoverability, providing a straightforward and modern shell experience.

While Fish may not be as customizable as Bash or Zsh, it offers a pleasant and efficient interactive shell environment.

Ksh (Korn Shell):
Ksh is a shell that combines features from both the Bourne and C shells (sh and csh).

It provides advanced scripting capabilities and interactive features, making it suitable for both interactive use and scripting.

Ksh includes features like command history, job control, and built-in arithmetic operations.

There are different variants of Ksh, such as ksh88, ksh93, and the open-source version, OpenKsh.

Csh (C Shell) and Tcsh (Enhanced C Shell):
Csh is a shell known for its C-like syntax and interactive features.
Tcsh is an enhanced version of Csh, providing additional features and improvements.
Csh and Tcsh offer command-line editing, history, and job control similar to Bash but with a different syntax and set of features.
While Csh and Tcsh are not as widely used as Bash or Zsh, they still find applications in certain Unix environments.
The choice of shell depends on personal preferences, specific needs, and the requirements of the task at hand.
Bash is generally recommended for compatibility and widespread support, while Zsh and Fish offer advanced interactive features and customization options. However, all shells provide the essential capabilities of a command-line interface, allowing users to run commands, manage processes, and execute shell scripts. Users can select and customise their preferred shell based on their workflow and preferences.

Shell Variables

In Linux and Unix-based operating systems, shell variables are used to store data that can be accessed and manipulated by the shell and shell scripts. Variables provide a way to store information temporarily or persistently and are used to customise the behaviour of the shell and its executed commands. Here's an overview of shell variables:

Variable Naming:
Shell variables are typically named using uppercase letters, numbers, or underscores.
They must start with a letter or an underscore, and they are case-sensitive.
Avoid using reserved keywords or special characters that may cause issues.

Assigning Values to Variables:
Variables are assigned values using the = operator, without any spaces around it.
For example, variable_name=value assigns the value to the variable.

Accessing Variable Values:
To access the value of a variable, precede its name with a $ symbol.
For example, echo $variable_name will display the value of the variable.

Predefined Variables:

The shell provides several predefined variables that contain useful information.
Examples of predefined variables:
$HOME: The current user's home directory.
$PATH: The search path for executable files.
$PWD: The current working directory.
$USER: The current username.

Environment Variables:

Environment variables are global variables that can be accessed by all processes.
They are typically defined in configuration files like .bashrc or by the system during startup.
Environment variables can be accessed and modified by shell scripts and affect the behaviour of commands and programs.
Common environment variables include $PATH, $HOME, and $LANG.

Local Variables:

Local variables are specific to a particular shell session or script.
They are created and accessed within the current shell session or script and are not accessible by other processes or sessions.
Local variables are useful for storing temporary or intermediate data.

Exporting Variables:
By default, variables created within a shell session are not visible to child processes.
To make a variable accessible to child processes, it needs to be exported using the export command.
For example, export variable_name exports the variable to the environment.

Modifying Variable Values:
Variable values can be modified using various operations like concatenation, substitution, and arithmetic calculations. The += operator is used for concatenation, and the ${} syntax allows substitution and manipulation of variable values.
Arithmetic calculations can be performed using the expr command or the $(( )) syntax.

Unsetting Variables:
Variables can be unset using the unset command, which removes the variable and its value from the shell environment.
For example, unset variable_name unsets the specified variable.
Shell variables are essential for customization, configuration, and automation in Linux and Unix-based systems. They allow users to store and manipulate data,

control the behaviour of the shell and its executed commands, and provide a way to pass information between processes and scripts. Understanding how to work with variables is fundamental for shell scripting and efficient command-line usage.

Writing and Running Shell Scripts

Shell scripts are files containing a sequence of shell commands that can be executed to automate tasks or perform a series of operations. Writing and running shell scripts is an efficient way to automate repetitive tasks and streamline command-line operations. Here's an overview of writing and running shell scripts:

Creating a Shell Script:
Create a new file with a .sh extension, such as script.sh, to indicate it as a shell script.
Use a text editor to open the file and start writing the shell commands.
The first line of the script should specify the shell to be used, known as the shebang. For example:
shell
#!/bin/bash

Write the desired commands in the subsequent lines of the script.

Adding Comments:
Comments provide explanations or documentation within the script and are not executed as commands.
Use the # symbol to indicate a comment. Everything after the # symbol on a line is considered a comment.

Making the Script Executable:
Before running a shell script, it needs to have executable permissions.
Use the chmod command to make the script executable. For example:
shell
chmod +x script.sh

Running the Shell Script:
To execute a shell script, use the following command format:
shell
Copy code
./script.sh
The ./ indicates that the script should be executed from the current directory.

Passing Arguments to a Shell Script:

Shell scripts can accept command-line arguments, allowing for customization and dynamic behaviour.
Within the script, arguments are accessed using special variables like $1, $2, etc., where $1 represents the first argument, $2 represents the second, and so on.
For example, the following script expects two arguments and displays them:
shell
#!/bin/bash
echo "First Argument: $1"
echo "Second Argument: $2"

Redirecting Output:
Shell scripts can redirect output to files or other commands using redirection operators.
The > operator redirects output to a file, overwriting its contents if the file exists. For example:
shell
echo "Hello, world!" > output.txt
The >> operator appends output to a file, preserving existing contents. For example:
shell
echo "Additional content" >> output.txt
Pipes (|) can be used to redirect output to another command. For example:
shell
ls -l | grep ".txt"

Control Flow and Looping:
Shell scripts support control flow statements like if, for, while, and case to handle conditional logic and looping. Conditional statements allow you to execute commands based on certain conditions.
Looping constructs enable repetitive execution of commands.

Exiting the Script:
To exit a script before it reaches the end, use the exit command followed by an optional exit code. For example:
shell
exit 0

Chapter eight

Writing and Running Shell Scripts

Shell scripts are files containing a sequence of shell commands that can be executed to automate tasks or perform a series of operations. Writing and running shell scripts is an efficient way to automate repetitive tasks and streamline command-line operations. Here's an overview of writing and running shell scripts:

Creating a Shell Script:
Create a new file with a .sh extension, such as script.sh, to indicate it as a shell script.
Use a text editor to open the file and start writing the shell commands.
The first line of the script should specify the shell to be used, known as the shebang. For example:
shell
#!/bin/bash
Write the desired commands in the subsequent lines of the scripts

Adding Comments:
Comments provide explanations or documentation within the script and are not executed as commands.

Use the # symbol to indicate a comment. Everything after the # symbol on a line is considered a comment.

Making the Script Executable:

Before running a shell script, it needs to have executable permissions.

Use the chmod command to make the script executable. For example:

shell

chmod +x script.sh

Running the Shell Script:

To execute a shell script, use the following command format:

shell

./script.sh

The ./ indicates that the script should be executed from the current directory.

Passing Arguments to a Shell Script:

Shell scripts can accept command-line arguments, allowing for customization and dynamic behaviour.

Within the script, arguments are accessed using special variables like $1, $2, etc., where $1 represents the first argument, $2 represents the second, and so on.

For example, the following script expects two arguments and displays them:

shell

#!/bin/bash

echo "First Argument: $1"

echo "Second Argument: $2"

Redirecting Output:

Shell scripts can redirect output to files or other commands using redirection operators.

The > operator redirects output to a file, overwriting its contents if the file exists. For example:

shell

echo "Hello, world!" > output.txt

The >> operator appends output to a file, preserving existing contents. For example:

shell

echo "Additional content" >> output.txt

Pipes (|) can be used to redirect output to another command. For example:

shell

ls -l | grep ".txt"

Control Flow and Looping:

Shell scripts support control flow statements like if, for, while, and case to handle conditional logic and looping.

Conditional statements allow you to execute commands based on certain conditions.

Looping constructs enable repetitive execution of commands.

Exiting the Script:

To exit a script before it reaches the end, use the exit command followed by an optional exit code. For example:

shell

exit 0

Shell scripting provides a powerful means of automating tasks, executing complex operations, and enhancing command-line productivity. With the ability to write custom scripts, users can create personalised workflows, automate repetitive tasks, and solve specific problems efficiently. Understanding the syntax, control flow, and available commands allows users to harness the full potential of shell scripting.

File Manipulation and Text Processing
In Linux and Unix-based systems, file manipulation and text processing are common tasks performed through the command line. Understanding various commands and techniques can help users efficiently manage and manipulate files and process text. Here's an overview of file manipulation and text processing in Linux:

Creating and Deleting Files:
The touch command creates an empty file. For example, touch myfile.txt.
The rm command deletes files. Use rm -r to remove directories and their contents recursively.
Copying and Moving Files:

The cp command is used to copy files. For example, cp file.txt destination/ copies file.txt to the destination directory.
The mv command moves files. Use it to rename files or move them to a different directory. For example, mv file.txt newname.txt renames the file.

Listing and Viewing Files:
The ls command lists files and directories in a directory. Use options like -l for a detailed listing or -a to display hidden files.
The cat command displays the contents of a file. For example, cat myfile.txt.

The less command allows scrolling and navigating through large text files.

Searching and Filtering Text:
The grep command searches for patterns in files. For example, grep "keyword" myfile.txt searches for the keyword in the file.
The sed command is used for text substitution and manipulation. For example, sed 's/old/new/g' myfile.txt replaces all occurrences of "old" with "new" in the file.
The awk command is a versatile text-processing tool. It processes files line by line and allows complex operations.

Sorting and Rearranging Text:
The sort command sorts lines of text alphabetically or numerically. For example, sort myfile.txt.
The cut command extracts specific columns or fields from lines of text. For example, cut -d "," -f 1 myfile.csv extracts the first column from a comma-separated file.
The head command displays the first few lines of a file, while tail displays the last few lines.

File Permissions and Ownership:
The chmod command changes file permissions. For example, chmod +x script.sh makes a script executable.
The chown command changes file ownership. For example, chown user myfile.txt changes the owner of the file to "user".

Archiving and Compression:
AThe tar command is used to create archives and extract files from them. For example, tar -cvf archive.tar files/ creates an archive of the "files" directory.

The gzip and gunzip commands compress and decompress files. For example, gzip myfile.txt compresses the file, creating myfile.txt.gz.

File Permissions and Ownership:
The chmod command changes file permissions. For example, chmod +x script.sh makes a script executable.
The chown command changes file ownership. For example, chown user myfile.txt changes the owner of the file to "user".
These are just a few examples of file manipulation and text processing in Linux. The command-line tools provide a wide range of options and flexibility to accomplish various tasks efficiently. By combining different commands and techniques, users can manipulate files, process text, and automate tasks to suit their specific needs.

Working with Files and Directories

In Linux and Unix-based systems, working with files and directories is a fundamental aspect of managing data and organising the file system. Understanding the essential commands and techniques for file and directory operations is crucial for efficient command-line usage. Here's an overview of working with files and directories in Linux:

File and Directory Navigation:

The cd command is used to navigate between directories. For example, cd /path/to/directory changes the current directory to the specified path.
The pwd command displays the present working directory, showing the current directory's full path.

Listing Files and Directories:
The ls command lists files and directories in the current directory. Use options like -l for a detailed listing or -a to display hidden files.
The tree command displays the directory structure in a tree-like format.

Creating and Deleting Files:
The touch command creates an empty file. For example, touch myfile.txt creates a file named myfile.txt.
The rm command deletes files. Use rm -r to remove directories and their contents recursively.

Creating and Deleting Directories:
The mkdir command creates directories. For example, mkdir mydir creates a directory named mydir.
The rmdir command deletes empty directories. Use rm -r to remove directories and their contents recursively.

Copying and Moving Files and Directories:
The cp command is used to copy files and directories. For example, cp file.txt destination/ copies file.txt to the destination directory.

The mv command moves files and directories. Use it to rename files or move them to a different directory. For example, mv file.txt newname.txt renames the file.

File Permissions and Ownership:
The chmod command changes file permissions. For example, chmod +x script.sh makes a script executable.
The chown command changes file ownership. For example, chown user myfile.txt changes the owner of the file to "user".

Finding Files:
The find command searches for files and directories based on various criteria like name, size, or permissions. For example, find /path -name myfile.txt searches for a file named myfile.txt in the specified path.

File Compression and Extraction:
The tar command is used to create archives and extract files from them. For example, tar -cvf archive.tar files/ creates an archive of the "files" directory.
The gzip and gunzip commands compress and decompress files. For example, gzip myfile.txt compresses the file, creating myfile.txt.gz.

Disk Usage:

The du command displays disk usage information for files and directories. Use options like -h for human-readable output or -s for summary.

Working with files and directories is a core skill in Linux. The commands mentioned above provide the necessary tools to navigate the file system, create, delete, and manipulate files and directories, change permissions, and search for files based on various criteria. Mastering these operations empowers users to efficiently manage their data and organise the file system according to their requirements.

Text Processing Tools: grep, sed, awk

In Linux and Unix-based systems, text processing plays a vital role in analysing, manipulating, and extracting information from files and streams. Several powerful command-line tools are widely used for text processing, including grep, sed, and awk. Here's an overview of these tools and their common applications:

grep:
The grep command is used for searching and filtering text based on patterns.

Syntax: grep [options] pattern [files]
Common options:
-i: Ignore case while matching.
-v: Invert the match, displaying lines that don't match the pattern.
-r: Recursively search directories.
Example usage:
grep "keyword" file.txt: Search for lines containing "keyword" in the file.
grep -i "case" file.txt: Search for lines containing "case" while ignoring case.

sed:
The sed command is a stream editor for text manipulation and transformation.
Syntax: sed [options] 'command' [file]
Common commands:
s/pattern/replacement/: Substitute a pattern with a replacement.
d: Delete lines that match a pattern.
p: Print lines that match a pattern.
Example usage:
sed 's/foo/bar/g' file.txt: Replace all occurrences of "foo" with "bar" in the file.
sed '/pattern/d' file.txt: Delete lines that match the pattern in the file.

awk:

The awk command is a versatile text-processing tool for pattern scanning and processing.

Syntax: awk 'pattern { action }' [file]

Common patterns and actions:

/pattern/: Matches lines containing the pattern.

{ print }: Prints the entire line.

{ print $1 }: Prints the first field of the line.

{ sum += $1 } END { print sum }: Calculates the sum of the first field and prints it at the end.

Example usage:

awk '/pattern/ { print }' file.txt: Print lines containing the pattern in the file.

awk '{ print $2 }' file.txt: Print the second field of each line in the file.

These text processing tools provide powerful capabilities for searching, filtering, substituting, and manipulating text in files and streams. By combining them with regular expressions and other command-line utilities, users can efficiently process and extract relevant information from text-based data. Familiarising yourself with grep, sed, and awk empowers you to perform complex text processing tasks effectively.

Chapter nine

Networking in Linux

Networking is a crucial aspect of any modern operating system, and Linux provides a robust set of tools and utilities for networking-related tasks. From configuring network interfaces to troubleshooting network connectivity, understanding networking in Linux is essential for system administrators and users alike. Here's an overview of networking in Linux:

Network Configuration:
The ifconfig command is used to configure network interfaces, display their configuration, or bring them up or down.
The ip command, which is more powerful and versatile, provides extensive functionality for network configuration, such as assigning IP addresses, managing routes, and manipulating network namespaces.

Network Interfaces:
Network interfaces in Linux are represented by devices like eth0, wlan0, lo (loopback), etc. They connect the system to a network or network devices.

The ifconfig or ip commands can be used to display information about network interfaces, enable or disable them, assign IP addresses, and configure other parameters.

Network Connectivity:
The ping command is used to check network connectivity to a specific IP address or hostname. It sends ICMP Echo Request packets and waits for ICMP Echo Reply packets to verify reachability.
The traceroute command traces the route packets take from the source to the destination, showing the IP addresses of intermediate hops.
The netstat command provides information about network connections, open ports, and routing tables. Use options like -t for TCP connections or -u for UDP connections.

DNS Configuration:
The /etc/resolv.conf file contains DNS server configuration. You can manually edit this file to specify DNS servers, search domains, and other DNS-related settings.
The nslookup command is used to query DNS servers to obtain information about domain names or IP addresses.

Firewall Configuration:

Linux includes several firewall management tools, such as iptables and ufw (Uncomplicated Firewall), for configuring network packet filtering and firewall rules.
These tools allow you to define rules to allow or deny network traffic based on various criteria like source IP, destination port, or protocol.

Network Services:
Linux supports a wide range of network services like SSH (Secure Shell), FTP (File Transfer Protocol), HTTP (Hypertext Transfer Protocol), etc. These services can be installed and configured to provide network functionality and remote access to the system.

Network Diagnostics and Troubleshooting:
The ifconfig, ip, ping, traceroute, and netstat commands mentioned earlier can be valuable for diagnosing network issues and troubleshooting network connectivity problems. The tcpdump command captures and analyses network traffic, allowing you to inspect packets and identify potential issues.

Networking in Linux encompasses a vast array of tools and utilities to configure network interfaces, troubleshoot connectivity problems, manage network services, and secure the system. Understanding these tools and their usage empowers administrators and users to effectively manage and troubleshoot network-related tasks on Linux systems.

Network Configuration

Configuring the network in a Linux system involves setting up network interfaces, assigning IP addresses, configuring DNS servers, and managing other network-related settings. Proper network configuration ensures connectivity and enables the system to communicate with other devices on the network. Here are the key aspects of network configuration in Linux:

Network Interface Configuration:

Network interfaces, such as Ethernet (eth0) or wireless (wlan0), connect the system to the network.

The configuration files for network interfaces are located in the /etc/network/interfaces or /etc/sysconfig/network-scripts directory, depending on the Linux distribution.

Typical network interface configuration involves specifying parameters like IP address, netmask, gateway, and DNS servers.

IP Address Configuration:

An IP address is a unique identifier assigned to each device on a network.

IP address configuration can be done manually or automatically through DHCP (Dynamic Host Configuration Protocol).

To configure IP addresses manually, modify the network interface configuration file and specify the desired IP address, netmask, and gateway.

DHCP Configuration:
DHCP allows automatic IP address assignment to systems on a network.
The configuration file for the DHCP client is typically located at /etc/dhcp/dhclient.conf.
DHCP configuration enables the system to obtain an IP address, subnet mask, default gateway, and DNS server information automatically from a DHCP server.

DNS Configuration:
DNS (Domain Name System) resolves domain names to IP addresses.
DNS configuration involves specifying DNS servers that the system should use for name resolution.
The DNS server configuration is typically defined in the /etc/resolv.conf file. However, some distributions may use other files or utilities to manage DNS configuration.

Network Manager:
Network Manager is a popular network configuration tool available in many Linux distributions.
It provides a graphical interface and command-line tools to manage network connections, including wired, wireless, and VPN connections.
Network Manager simplifies the process of configuring and managing network interfaces, DHCP, DNS, and other network-related settings.

Network Restart and Service Management:
After making changes to network configuration files, it's necessary to restart the network service for the changes to take effect.
The commands for restarting the network service vary depending on the Linux distribution. For example, systemctl restart network or service networking restart. Proper network configuration is crucial for establishing connectivity and enabling communication between systems on a network. Whether configuring network interfaces manually or using DHCP, ensuring accurate IP address assignment, gateway configuration, and DNS settings is vital. Network Manager provides a convenient way to manage network connections for both desktop and server environments. By understanding network configuration principles and tools, administrators and users can effectively set up and manage network connectivity in Linux systems.

IP Addressing and Subnetting

IP addressing is a fundamental concept in computer networking that allows devices to communicate with each other over IP-based networks. IP addresses uniquely identify devices on a network and facilitate data transmission. Subnetting, on the other hand, is the process of dividing a network into smaller subnetworks, enabling efficient address allocation and network management. Here's an overview of IP addressing and subnetting in the context of Linux networking:

IP Address Basics:
An IP address is a 32-bit numeric identifier assigned to each device on a network. It consists of four octets (e.g., 192.168.0.1), where each octet represents 8 bits.
IP addresses are divided into two parts: network and host portions. The network portion identifies the network to which the device belongs, while the host portion identifies the specific device on the network.

IP Address Classes:
IP addresses were traditionally divided into five classes: A, B, C, D, and E.
Class A addresses have a range of 1.0.0.0 to 126.255.255.255 and are typically used for large networks.
Class B addresses have a range of 128.0.0.0 to 191.255.255.255 and are used for medium-sized networks.
Class C addresses have a range of 192.0.0.0 to 223.255.255.255 and are commonly used for small networks.
Class D addresses (224.0.0.0 to 239.255.255.255) are reserved for multicasting.
Class E addresses (240.0.0.0 to 255.255.255.255) are reserved for future use.

Private IP Addresses:
Private IP addresses are reserved for use within private networks and are not routable on the public internet.
The most commonly used private IP address ranges are:
Class A: 10.0.0.0 to 10.255.255.255
Class B: 172.16.0.0 to 172.31.255.255
Class C: 192.168.0.0 to 192.168.255.255
Private IP addresses enable organisations to create their own internal networks without requiring unique public IP addresses for each device.

Subnetting:
Subnetting allows network administrators to divide a large network into smaller subnetworks (subnets) for improved address allocation and network management.
Subnetting involves borrowing bits from the host portion of an IP address to create a subnet mask.
The subnet mask determines the network and host portions of an IP address. It consists of a series of 1s followed by a series of 0s.
Common subnet mask notations include:
CIDR (Classless Inter-Domain Routing) notation, e.g., /24 for a 24-bit subnet mask.
Dotted Decimal notation, e.g., 255.255.255.0 for a 24-bit subnet mask.

Network Address and Broadcast Address:
Each subnet has a network address and a broadcast address. The network address is the first address in the subnet and represents the subnet itself.

The broadcast address is the last address in the subnet and is used to send a broadcast message to all devices in the subnet.

Understanding IP addressing and subnetting is essential for network design, addressing allocation, and network troubleshooting. Proper subnetting allows for efficient utilisation of IP addresses and helps in organising and managing networks effectively. By mastering IP addressing and subnetting concepts, network administrators can optimise network performance, enhance security, and facilitate seamless communication among devices on the network.

Common Network Utilities

Network utilities are essential tools used for network administration, troubleshooting, and monitoring. These utilities provide valuable information about network connectivity, diagnose network issues, and aid in optimising network performance. In a Linux environment, there are several common network utilities available. Here are some of the most widely used ones:

Ping:
The ping command is used to test network connectivity between two devices. It sends ICMP Echo Request packets to a specified IP address or hostname and waits for ICMP Echo Reply packets.
Ping is useful for checking if a remote device is reachable and measuring round-trip time (RTT) between devices.

Traceroute:
The traceroute command helps trace the path that packets take from the source device to a specified destination device or hostname.
Traceroute displays the IP addresses of intermediate hops along with the round-trip time (RTT) for each hop.
This utility helps identify network bottlenecks, latency issues, or packet loss within the network.

Netstat:
The netstat command provides information about active network connections, listening ports, and routing tables.

It displays details such as the source and destination IP addresses, protocol used (TCP or UDP), state of the connection, and port numbers.
Netstat is useful for monitoring network connections, identifying open ports, and troubleshooting network-related issues.

Nslookup:
The nslookup command is used to query DNS (Domain Name System) servers to obtain information about domain names or IP addresses.
It helps in troubleshooting DNS-related problems, verifying DNS configurations, and resolving domain names to IP addresses.

Nmap:
Nmap (Network Mapper) is a powerful network scanning tool used for port scanning, host discovery, and OS detection.
It provides detailed information about open ports, services running on those ports, and the operating system of the target device.
Nmap is commonly used for security assessments, network inventory, and network mapping.

Tcpdump:
Tcpdump is a command-line packet analyzer that captures and analyses network traffic in real-time.

It allows network administrators to inspect packets, filter packets based on various criteria, and identify network anomalies or malicious activity.

Tcpdump is a versatile tool for troubleshooting network issues, monitoring network traffic, and performing network analysis.

Wireshark:

Wireshark is a powerful network protocol analyzer with a graphical user interface (GUI).

It captures and analyses network packets in real-time and provides detailed information about protocols, packet contents, and network behaviour.

Wireshark is widely used for network troubleshooting, protocol analysis, and network forensics.

These common network utilities are invaluable for network administrators and IT professionals to diagnose network problems, analyse network behaviour, and ensure optimal network performance. By utilising these tools effectively, administrators can maintain a stable and secure network environment.

Chapter ten

System Monitoring and Maintenance

System monitoring and maintenance are crucial tasks in Linux to ensure optimal performance, troubleshoot issues, and keep the system secure. By monitoring various system parameters and performing regular maintenance tasks, administrators can identify potential problems, optimise system resources, and ensure the stability of the Linux environment. Here are some key aspects of system monitoring and maintenance:

Performance Monitoring:
Monitoring system performance helps administrators identify resource bottlenecks, optimise system utilisation, and ensure smooth operation.
Tools like top, htop, and glances provide real-time monitoring of system resources such as CPU usage, memory usage, disk I/O, and network activity.
Performance monitoring tools also enable tracking of process-specific resource utilisation, helping identify resource-intensive processes.

Log Monitoring:

Logs contain valuable information about system events, errors, and warnings. Monitoring logs helps in identifying issues, troubleshooting problems, and ensuring system security.

The /var/log/ directory stores various logs, such as system logs (/var/log/syslog), authentication logs (/var/log/auth.log), and application-specific logs.

Tools like tail, grep, and journalctl are used to monitor and search through log files, allowing administrators to track system events and detect anomalies.

Disk Space Monitoring:

Monitoring disk space usage is essential to prevent disk overflow, ensure system availability, and maintain proper storage capacity.

Commands like df and du help monitor disk usage at the file system level, providing information on available space, used space, and utilisation by individual directories and files.

Setting up automated alerts or scripts to monitor disk space can proactively notify administrators when the disk utilisation exceeds predefined thresholds.

System Updates and Patch Management:

Keeping the Linux system up to date with the latest security patches and software updates is crucial for maintaining system security and stability.

Tools like apt, yum, or dnf are package managers that handle updates and patch management in Debian-based,

Red Hat-based, and Fedora-based distributions, respectively.

Regularly applying security patches and updates ensures that vulnerabilities are addressed and system performance is optimised.

User and Access Management:

Monitoring user accounts, access privileges, and login activity is important for maintaining system security and preventing unauthorised access.

Commands like who, last, and w provide information about active user sessions and login history.

Regularly reviewing user accounts, disabling unnecessary accounts, and enforcing strong password policies help protect the system from unauthorised access.

Backup and Recovery:

Regularly backing up critical system files, user data, and configurations is essential to ensure data integrity and facilitate system recovery in case of failures or disasters. Tools like rsync, tar, or backup solutions like Bacula and Amanda enable automated backup of files and directories. Testing backups periodically and implementing a robust backup strategy ensures data availability and minimise downtime during recovery scenarios.

Security Monitoring:

Monitoring system security involves detecting and responding to security threats, vulnerabilities, and intrusions.

Security monitoring tools like fail2ban, logwatch, and intrusion detection systems (IDS) help identify suspicious activities, log anomalies, and potential security breaches. Regular security audits, vulnerability assessments, and penetration testing contribute to a proactive security posture.

System monitoring and maintenance tasks should be performed regularly to ensure system health, optimise performance, and enhance system security. By leveraging the appropriate monitoring tools, performing routine maintenance tasks, and staying vigilant about system security, administrators can maintain a stable and reliable Linux environment.

Process Management

Process management is an essential aspect of Linux administration, involving the monitoring, control, and optimization of processes running on a system. Understanding how processes work and effectively managing them ensures efficient resource utilisation and system stability. Here are key aspects of process management in Linux:

Process Basics:
A process is an instance of a running program. It consists of executable code, memory, and system resources required for its execution.
Each process is assigned a unique process ID (PID) that helps identify and manage it.
Processes can run in the foreground (interactively) or in the background (without user interaction).

Process States:
Processes in Linux can exist in various states, including:
Running: The process is actively executing on the CPU.
Sleeping: The process is waiting for an event or resource.
Stopped: The process has been paused or stopped, often by a user or a signal.
Zombie: The process has completed execution but still has an entry in the process table until its parent acknowledges its termination.

Process Monitoring:
Tools like ps, top, and htop provide real-time monitoring of processes.
The ps command lists active processes along with their status, resource utilisation, and parent-child relationships.
top and htop display an interactive dynamic view of processes, CPU usage, memory usage, and system statistics.

Process Control:

The kill command is used to send signals to processes. The default signal is SIGTERM, which requests a process to terminate gracefully.

Commonly used signals include SIGKILL (terminate immediately), SIGHUP (hang-up), SIGSTOP (pause), and SIGCONT (resume).

The killall command can terminate multiple processes based on their names or other criteria.

Process Prioritisation:

Processes have priority levels that determine their access to system resources, such as CPU time.

The nice command is used to adjust the priority of a process. Higher niceness values indicate lower priority.

The renice command allows changing the priority of running processes.

Process Termination:

Processes can be terminated gracefully or forcefully if necessary.

Graceful termination involves sending a SIGTERM signal to the process, allowing it to clean up resources and exit gracefully.

In cases of unresponsive or problematic processes, a SIGKILL signal can be sent using the kill command to force termination.

Process Scheduling:

Linux uses scheduling algorithms to determine the order in which processes are executed. The nice value affects the scheduling priority of a process. Lower values indicate higher priority. Tools like chrt can be used to set real-time scheduling policies for critical processes. Effective process management is vital for optimising system performance, resource allocation, and stability. Monitoring process activity, controlling processes, and understanding process states contribute to efficient system administration. By managing processes effectively, administrators can ensure smooth system operation and enhance overall system performance.

System Performance Monitoring

System performance monitoring is a critical aspect of Linux administration that involves tracking and analysing various metrics to ensure optimal system operation, detect bottlenecks, and identify areas for improvement. By monitoring system performance, administrators can proactively address issues, optimise resource utilisation, and maintain a stable and efficient Linux environment. Here are key aspects of system performance monitoring:

CPU Utilisation:

Monitoring CPU utilisation helps determine the workload on the processor and identify processes or applications that consume excessive CPU resources.

Tools like top, htop, and sar provide real-time and historical CPU usage information, including overall CPU utilisation, individual process utilisation, and system load averages.

Memory Utilisation:
Monitoring memory usage is crucial to ensure efficient utilisation of available memory and avoid excessive swapping that can degrade system performance.
Tools like free, top, and sar display information about total memory, used memory, free memory, and memory usage by processes.
Monitoring memory utilisation helps identify memory-intensive processes and optimise memory allocation.

Disk I/O:
Monitoring disk I/O activity helps identify performance bottlenecks and optimise disk usage.
Tools like iostat, iotop, and sar provide information on disk read and write rates, I/O wait times, and disk utilisation.
Monitoring disk I/O helps identify processes or storage devices causing high disk activity and optimise I/O performance.

Network Utilisation:
Monitoring network utilisation allows administrators to identify network congestion, bandwidth utilisation, and potential network-related issues.

Tools like ifconfig, nethogs, and sar provide insights into network interfaces, traffic statistics, and bandwidth usage. Monitoring network utilisation helps optimise network performance, detect abnormal network traffic, and identify potential network bottlenecks.

System Load:
System load reflects the number of processes in the system's run queue waiting to be executed. High system load can indicate resource contention or insufficient system capacity.
The uptime command provides system load averages for the last 1, 5, and 15 minutes.
Monitoring system load helps assess system performance and capacity requirements.

Process Monitoring:
Monitoring individual processes helps identify resource-intensive or misbehaving processes that may impact system performance.
Tools like top, htop, and ps provide real-time process information, including CPU and memory utilisation.
Monitoring processes helps detect issues like excessive resource consumption, stuck processes, or memory leaks.

Log Analysis:

Analysing system logs provides valuable insights into system behaviour, errors, and warnings that can impact performance.
Tools like grep, awk, and logwatch help search, filter, and analyse log files for specific patterns or anomalies.
Analysing logs helps identify system issues, performance degradation, or security-related events.

Performance Trend Analysis:
Collecting and analysing performance data over time helps identify long-term trends, patterns, and potential issues.
Tools like sar, munin, and Zabbix enable performance data collection and graphing for historical analysis.
Performance trend analysis helps identify performance degradation, plan capacity upgrades, and optimise system resources.
System performance monitoring is an ongoing process that requires regular monitoring, analysis, and optimization. By monitoring and analysing key performance metrics, administrators can proactively address performance issues, optimise resource utilisation, and ensure a stable and efficient Linux environment.

Log Files and System Logging

Log files and system logging play a vital role in Linux administration by capturing important system events, errors, warnings, and other relevant information. Understanding log files and effectively utilising system logging mechanisms is crucial for troubleshooting issues, monitoring system health, and ensuring the security and stability of a Linux environment. Here are key aspects of log files and system logging:

Log Files:
Log files are text files that store records of system events, activities, and messages.
Various log files exist in different locations on the Linux system, such as /var/log/ directory, containing logs from different subsystems and applications.
Common log files include:
System logs: /var/log/syslog, /var/log/messages, /var/log/kern.log.
Authentication logs: /var/log/auth.log (Debian-based systems), /var/log/secure (Red Hat-based systems).
Application-specific logs: Apache web server logs (/var/log/apache2/access.log, /var/log/apache2/error.log), MySQL database logs, etc.

System Logging:
System logging is the process of capturing and recording system events and messages generated by the kernel, applications, and services.

Linux systems use a logging framework, such as the syslogd daemon or its replacements (rsyslogd or systemd-journald), to manage system logging.
The logging framework receives messages and categorises them into different log files based on their severity and facility.

Log Levels and Severity:
Log messages are categorised into different levels or severity levels, indicating their importance and urgency.
Common log levels include:
Emergency: Indicates a system-wide catastrophic failure.
Alert: Indicates a condition that requires immediate attention.
Critical: Indicates a critical condition that requires action.
Error: Indicates an error condition but not critical.
Warning: Indicates a potential issue or abnormal condition.
Notice: Indicates normal but significant events.
Informational: Provides informative messages about system activities.
Debug: Provides detailed debugging information.

Logging Facilities:
Logging facilities categorise messages based on the source or subsystem generating them.
Common logging facilities include:
Kernel messages: Logs generated by the Linux kernel.
User-level messages: Logs generated by user-level applications and services.

Mail messages: Logs related to mail server activities.
Authentication messages: Logs related to user authentication and login activities.
System daemons: Logs generated by system daemons like cron, systemd, etc.

Log Rotation:
Log rotation is the process of managing log files to prevent them from growing too large and consuming excessive disk space.
Log rotation utilities, such as logrotate, automate the compression, archival, and deletion of old log files.
Log rotation helps ensure efficient log management and prevents log files from overwhelming the system.

Log Analysis and Monitoring:
Analysing and monitoring log files provide valuable insights into system behaviour, errors, and warnings.
Tools like grep, awk, sed, and log analysis tools like ELK stack or Splunk help search, filter, and analyse log files for specific patterns or anomalies.
Log analysis and monitoring help in troubleshooting issues, identifying security threats, and detecting system anomalies.
Understanding log files and leveraging system logging mechanisms is essential for Linux administrators. Regularly reviewing and analysing log files can help identify system

issues, track events, troubleshoot problems, and ensure the security and stability of the Linux environment.

Chapter eleven

Troubleshooting and Debugging

Troubleshooting and debugging are essential skills for Linux administrators to identify and resolve issues that arise in the system. By employing systematic approaches and utilising various tools and techniques, administrators can effectively diagnose and fix problems, ensuring the smooth operation of the Linux environment. Here are key aspects of troubleshooting and debugging in Linux:

Problem Identification:
The first step in troubleshooting is identifying the problem. This involves gathering information about the symptoms, error messages, and any recent changes to the system or software.
System logs, error messages, and user reports are valuable sources of information for problem identification.

Systematic Approach:
Troubleshooting is best approached systematically to avoid overlooking crucial details or making hasty assumptions.

A systematic approach may involve isolating the problem, reproducing the issue, and narrowing down potential causes.

Documentation and Research:
Documenting the troubleshooting process is important for future reference and sharing knowledge with other team members.
Researching the problem online, including forums, documentation, and knowledge bases, can provide insights and potential solutions.

Diagnostic Tools:
Linux offers a wide range of diagnostic tools for troubleshooting various aspects of the system.
Command-line tools like dmesg, top, htop, netstat, and lsof provide valuable information about system processes, resource usage, network connections, and open files.
System monitoring tools like sar and vmstat can help track system performance and identify bottlenecks.

Debugging Techniques:
Debugging involves analysing and resolving issues in software applications.

Techniques like logging, code inspection, and using debugging tools like gdb (GNU Debugger) help identify and fix software-related problems.
Debugging often requires understanding programming languages, stack traces, and application-specific debugging methods.

Kernel Debugging:
Kernel-related issues require advanced debugging techniques.
Tools like kgdb (Kernel GNU Debugger), kdump, and SystemTap help analyse kernel crashes, performance issues, and kernel module problems.

Configuration Errors:
Many issues arise due to misconfigurations in the system, applications, or services.
Double-checking configuration files and settings is crucial for resolving such issues.
Configuration management tools like Ansible, Chef, or Puppet can assist in maintaining consistent configurations across multiple systems.

Testing and Validation:
Testing changes or proposed solutions in a controlled environment helps verify their effectiveness and avoid potential side effects.

Creating test environments, using virtualization technologies like KVM or VirtualBox, facilitates safe testing without impacting production systems.

Collaboration and Documentation:
Troubleshooting often involves collaboration with colleagues or support communities.
Sharing knowledge and documenting the troubleshooting process, including the steps taken and their outcomes, helps build a knowledge base for future reference.

Regular Updates and Maintenance:
Keeping the system up to date with the latest software updates, security patches, and bug fixes helps prevent known issues and vulnerabilities.
Regular system maintenance, including disk cleanup, log rotation, and periodic health checks, can help identify and prevent potential issues.
Troubleshooting and debugging are iterative processes that require patience, attention to detail, and continuous learning. By employing systematic approaches, leveraging diagnostic tools, and collaborating with others, Linux administrators can effectively resolve issues, maintain system stability, and ensure a smooth user experience.

Common Linux Issues

Linux is a robust and reliable operating system, but like any complex software, it can experience certain issues from time to time. Understanding common Linux issues and knowing how to resolve them is essential for Linux administrators to maintain system stability and ensure smooth operations. Here are some of the most common Linux issues and their potential solutions:

Boot Failure:
One of the most critical issues is a failure to boot the system.
Common causes include misconfigured boot loaders, corrupt or missing boot files, or hardware failures.
Solutions may involve checking boot configurations, reinstalling boot loaders (e.g., GRUB), or diagnosing hardware issues.

Network Connectivity Issues:
Problems with network connectivity can disrupt communication and access to resources.
Issues may be related to misconfigured network interfaces, firewall settings, DNS resolution, or network hardware problems.
Troubleshooting involves verifying network configurations, checking connectivity (ping, traceroute), and examining firewall rules.

Software Installation and Dependencies:
Installing software and managing dependencies can sometimes lead to issues.
Problems may arise from incompatible library versions, missing dependencies, or conflicting package installations.
Solutions involve resolving dependency issues, ensuring proper package sources, and using package management tools effectively.

Application or Service Failures:
Application or service failures can occur due to software bugs, misconfigurations, or resource limitations.
Troubleshooting involves checking application logs, verifying configurations, and ensuring sufficient system resources (CPU, memory, disk space).

Filesystem Corruption:
Filesystem corruption can cause data loss or system instability.
Corruption can result from sudden power outages, hardware failures, or software bugs.
Recovery involves running filesystem repair tools (e.g., fsck) and restoring from backups if necessary.

Slow Performance:

Slow system performance can impact user experience and productivity.

Causes may include high CPU or memory usage, disk I/O bottlenecks, or inefficient software configurations.

Solutions involve identifying resource-intensive processes, optimising system configurations, and upgrading hardware if needed.

Security Vulnerabilities:

Linux systems can be vulnerable to security exploits and attacks.

Issues may include outdated software versions, misconfigured permissions, or weak passwords.

Resolutions involve keeping the system up to date with security patches, implementing proper permissions and access controls, and following security best practices.

User Account and Authentication Problems:

Issues related to user accounts and authentication can impact user access and system security.

Problems may include forgotten passwords, locked accounts, or incorrect authentication configurations.

Solutions involve resetting passwords, unlocking accounts, or adjusting authentication settings.

Disk Space Issues:

Insufficient disk space can lead to system errors and inability to store data.

Causes may include large log files, excessive software installations, or unmanaged file accumulation. Troubleshooting involves identifying and removing unnecessary files, managing log files, and resizing partitions if necessary.

Hardware Compatibility:
Linux may encounter compatibility issues with certain hardware components or peripherals.

Solutions involve researching and installing appropriate device drivers, updating firmware, or seeking community support for compatibility workarounds.

When encountering Linux issues, it's important to approach troubleshooting systematically, gather relevant information, and research possible solutions. Regular system maintenance, staying updated with security patches, and having backups in place are essential practices to prevent and mitigate common Linux issues. Additionally, engaging with the Linux community and forums can provide valuable insights and assistance when facing more complex problems.

Diagnosing and Fixing Problems

Diagnosing and fixing problems in a Linux environment is a critical skill for system administrators. When issues arise, having a structured approach to problem-solving can help identify the root cause and implement effective solutions. Here are some steps to diagnose and fix problems in a Linux system:

Define the Problem:
Clearly define the problem by identifying the symptoms, error messages, and any recent changes or actions that might have triggered the issue.
Gather information from users, system logs, and monitoring tools to gain a comprehensive understanding of the problem.

Reproduce the Problem:
Reproduce the problem if possible to observe the issue and understand its behaviour.
Identifying specific steps or conditions that trigger the problem can help narrow down potential causes.

Research and Analyze:
Research the issue by consulting documentation, online resources, and relevant forums or communities.
Analyse error messages, log files, and system configurations to identify patterns or known issues related to the problem.

Check System Resources:
Examine system resource utilisation, including CPU, memory, disk space, and network connectivity.
High resource usage or bottlenecks can lead to performance issues or service disruptions.

Test and Verify:
Perform tests to validate hypotheses and identify the scope of the problem.
Isolate the problem by testing different components, configurations, or scenarios to narrow down potential causes.

Debugging and Troubleshooting Tools:
Utilise debugging and troubleshooting tools available in Linux, such as strace, ltrace, or tcpdump, to gather more detailed information about processes, system calls, or network traffic.
Use log analysis tools like grep, awk, or specialised log parsers to extract relevant information from system logs.

Check System Configuration:

Review system configuration files, including network settings, services, and application configurations, for potential misconfigurations or conflicts.
Compare configurations with known working setups or backup configurations to identify discrepancies.

Rollback Recent Changes:
If the problem occurred after recent changes or updates, consider rolling back those changes to determine if they are the cause.
This can involve reverting configuration changes, downgrading software versions, or undoing system updates.

Apply Solutions:
Based on the analysis and research conducted, apply appropriate solutions to fix the problem.
Solutions may include applying software patches, modifying configuration settings, updating drivers, or reinstalling software components.

Test and Monitor:
After implementing solutions, thoroughly test the system to ensure the problem is resolved.
Monitor the system closely to verify that the issue does not reoccur and to identify any potential side effects of the applied solutions.

Document the Solution:

Document the problem, the steps taken for diagnosis and resolution, and any additional insights gained during the troubleshooting process.

This documentation serves as a knowledge base for future reference and helps other team members facing similar issues.

Remember, diagnosing and fixing problems in a Linux system often requires patience, attention to detail, and a systematic approach. Regular system maintenance, staying updated with software patches, and monitoring system health can help prevent issues from occurring in the first place. Additionally, active engagement with the Linux community and forums can provide valuable insights and assistance when tackling complex problems.

Useful Troubleshooting Tools

When it comes to troubleshooting issues in a Linux system, having the right set of tools at your disposal can greatly simplify the process. These tools help you gather information, analyse system behaviour, and identify the root causes of problems. Here are some useful troubleshooting tools commonly used in Linux environments:

Command-Line Tools:
top and htop: Monitor system resource usage, including CPU, memory, and processes.
dmesg: Display kernel ring buffer messages, useful for diagnosing hardware-related issues.
netstat and ss: Examine network connections, listening ports, and routing tables.
lsof: List open files and identify processes that have them open.
strace and ltrace: Trace system calls or library calls made by a process, aiding in debugging.

Log Analysis Tools:
grep, awk, and sed: Powerful command-line tools for searching, filtering, and manipulating text data, including log files.
journalctl: Query and analyse systemd journal logs, providing detailed information about system services and events.
tail and less: Display the last lines or scroll through log files in real-time.

Network Troubleshooting Tools:
ping: Test network connectivity to a specific host.
traceroute and mtr: Trace the route packets take to reach a destination, identifying network hops and latency.

tcpdump and Wireshark: Capture and analyse network packets for detailed network troubleshooting.

System Monitoring Tools:
sar and vmstat: Monitor system performance, including CPU usage, memory utilisation, and disk I/O statistics.
nmon and glances: Comprehensive system monitoring tools with real-time displays of key performance metrics.
iftop and nethogs: Monitor network traffic and identify bandwidth-consuming processes.

Disk and Filesystem Tools:
df and du: Display disk usage information, including available space and directory sizes.
smartctl: Monitor and analyse hard drive health and performance.
fsck: Filesystem consistency checker used to repair corrupted filesystems.

Remote Troubleshooting Tools:
ssh: Securely access remote systems and perform troubleshooting tasks.
rsync and scp: Transfer files securely between local and remote systems.

htop and top (with remote monitoring enabled): Monitor remote systems in real-time.

Debugging Tools:
gdb: The GNU Debugger allows you to analyse and debug programs at the source code level.
valgrind: Detect memory leaks, analyse program execution, and profile system performance.

Performance Monitoring Tools:
perf: Profiling tool for analysing system performance, including CPU and memory usage.
sysstat: Collection of tools that monitor system performance and generate historical reports.

System Information Tools:
uname: Display system information, including the kernel version, architecture, and hostname.
lshw and hwinfo: Retrieve detailed hardware information.

Package Management Tools:
apt (Debian-based systems) or dnf (Fedora-based systems): Package management tools for installing, updating, and removing software packages.

These are just a few examples of the numerous troubleshooting tools available in the Linux ecosystem. The choice of tools depends on the specific problem at hand and the information required for analysis. By becoming familiar with these tools and understanding their functionalities, you can efficiently diagnose and resolve issues, ensuring the smooth operation of your Linux systems.

Chapter twelve

conclusion

In this guide, we have covered the fundamental concepts of Linux for newcomers. Linux is a powerful and versatile operating system widely used in various domains, including servers, desktops, embedded systems, and more. Understanding the core concepts of Linux is essential for newcomers to navigate and work effectively in this environment.

We began with an introduction to Linux, exploring its history, features, and benefits. We then discussed how to get started with Linux, including choosing a distribution and setting up dual booting with Windows. We explored the Linux file system and the File Hierarchy Standard, gaining insights into the organisation and structure of files and directories.

Understanding file permissions and security is crucial in Linux, and we covered the concepts of file permissions, ownership, and access control. We also delved into navigating the file system using the command line interface, learning essential commands and techniques.

Terminal emulators and the various shell types, such as Bash and Zsh, were introduced to provide a comprehensive understanding of the command line interface. We explored shell variables, which allow for the storage and manipulation of data, as well as writing and running shell scripts for automation and task execution.

Package management and software repositories were discussed, emphasising the importance of managing software installations, updates, and dependencies. We covered common package managers, such as apt and yum, and highlighted the significance of maintaining system security through regular updates.

The topic of user and group management was covered, including creating and managing user accounts, as well as assigning permissions and access privileges. We also touched upon networking in Linux, network configuration, IP addressing, subnetting, and common network utilities for troubleshooting and analysis.

System monitoring and maintenance were addressed, focusing on process management, system performance monitoring, log files, and system logging. We explored security and permissions, highlighting the significance of securing the Linux environment and managing user access.

Lastly, we covered troubleshooting and debugging, discussing common Linux issues, and providing a structured approach to diagnosing and fixing problems. We introduced useful troubleshooting tools to aid in the troubleshooting process.

By gaining a solid foundation in these fundamental concepts of Linux, newcomers can confidently navigate the Linux environment, perform essential tasks, and effectively troubleshoot issues that may arise. Linux offers immense flexibility, scalability, and customization options, making it a preferred choice for both personal and professional use.

Remember, the journey with Linux is continuous, and there is always more to explore and learn. Keep exploring, practising, and engaging with the Linux community to expand your knowledge and expertise. Embrace the power of Linux, and enjoy the freedom it offers in the world of computing!

www.ingramcontent.com/pod-product-compliance
Lightning Source LLC
Chambersburg PA
CBHW071512220526
45472CB00003B/994